SKI
in a week

Ian McGarry, Camilla Buxton
and Tessa Coker

Headway · Hodder & Stoughton

ACKNOWLEDGEMENTS

The publishers would like to thank the following for their kind permission to use the photographs on pages: 1, 8, 54 Arthur Van Born; 14, Skishoot.

About the authors: Ian McGarry holds a BASI Grade 1 International Ski Instructor's licence, and trains and examines ski instructors. He runs his own ski clinics for the public, in the French Haute Savoie village of Chatel, where his qualifications as a club race trainer and coach in the 'inner game' techniques are incorporated into his own successful teaching methods – McGarry the ski system.
Camilla Buxton has lectured and reported on skiing topics for magazines and radio and was formerly publicity manager for the Ski Club of Great Britain.

Photographs by Mark Shapiro.

Illustrations by Jane McGarry, a BASI grade II instructor.

Author's Note: The information and instruction given in this book is divided into 'days' to make it easy to follow. It is not intended to suggest what you should do for each day of a seven day holiday.

British Library Cataloguing in Publication Data
McGarry, Ian
 Skiing in a week.
 1. Skiing
 I. Title   II. Buxton, Camilla
 796.93

ISBN 0 340 53513 x

Typeset and illustrated by Gecko Ltd, Bicester, Oxon
Printed in Great Britain for Headway, a division of Hodder and Stoughton Publishers, Mill Road, Dunton Green, Sevenoaks, Kent by Cambus Litho, East Kilbride.

CONTENTS

GETTING THE MOST FROM YOUR HOLIDAY

Skiing is fun! You are about to embark on learning a sport that will assure you of marvellous holidays for years to come.

Begin by giving careful consideration to the choice of your first ski resort. The success of your holiday, your enjoyment of the new experience of skiing, depends on good facilities for the beginner. What is the point, as a complete novice, in heading for a resort famed for its difficult slopes? There are many more resorts than those featured in 'Ski Sunday' as a glance at any ski brochure will tell you.

MONDAY

A first skiing holiday has to be approached with an open mind; see it more as a 'winter experience' holiday. Being out in the clean air of the mountains surrounded by spectacular scenery is a holiday in itself, quite apart from the invigoration of skiing. After all, your carefully laid plans to ski for seven days could be flawed by unexpected weather changes (skiing in a snow storm is not much fun) so while you are away be prepared to try your hand at other activities offered by the resort. You could skate, or go Curling. And don't forget to take a swimsuit!

Another point to remember as you leaf through the brochures is that splashing out on the highest priced holiday will not necessarily guarantee you the greatest enjoyment. Of course, to a certain extent (especially with accommodation) you 'get what you pay for'. But bear in mind that learning to ski *and* enjoying yourself can be achieved just as well, and often better, in a small, more modestly priced resort.

Making the right choice

The range of resorts on offer is bewildering, so concentrate on your requirements as a beginner before being side-tracked into a choice that may not suit you. It is most important that the resort has a good spread of easy runs and a selection of non-skiing activities for when skiing becomes too much or too exhausting, (exhaustion can be avoided by getting fit first). The list that follows will help in choosing a resort. Ask yourself:

What are the needs of your group?

Ski lessons

All beginners will need ski lessons. Don't for a minute let a friend persuade you that he can teach you, or worse still that you can learn all by yourself; it will take much longer and you will pick up bad habits. Head straight for the ski school and join the beginners class – unless you have already learnt the basics on a dry slope at home when you might be able to begin with a higher class. The more popular the resort with the British, the more likely it will be that the ski instructor speaks good English, so choose a resort that features in more than one brochure.

Small children

Those with families should note that many resorts are now well equipped for coping with small children or babies. Crêches for babies are often available, with some taking them as young as nine months, and safe play areas where young children can learn the basics of skiing by playing games in the snow on skis are now the norm. Skiing is such a good family pastime that more and more tour operators are offering a nanny and child care service.

If you are taking children remember to take some of their favourite toys because they may be miserable at first when finding themselves left with strangers in an unusual place. Make sure that they are warmly clothed and protected against the sun; too often parents forget to think about this – and a cold child is a miserable child.

Night life

An adult group will certainly wish to see a bit of the town's night life and these people might find the facilities of a very small hamlet limiting. Many resorts arrange local sport and entertainments for those who have the energy for other activities after skiing such as skating, tobogganing, cross-country skiing and swimming (which soothes muscular pain). Sports centres often have bars, in addition!

Other entertainment

A group of mixed skiers and non-skiers should choose a large resort with an established community and easy access to a town so that non-skiers (or those who want a break from skiing) have something to do other than meet the skiers and be bored by their tales of feats accomplished. Being abroad is also a chance to brush up on languages.

When to go

Price

At different times of year the price of packages and accommodation varies. Christmas and New Year, Easter and most of February (school half terms in Europe) are the most expensive. Mid January is the cheapest with March becoming progressively more expensive towards the week before Easter – few holidays are offered after Easter regardless of the date upon which it falls.

Snow

A normal winter season has a definite snow and temperature pattern; day temperatures become warmer from February onwards (it can be very cold for children before then), and snow cover and quality is normally best in mid-January to mid-March. Depending on the height of the actual ski area (which could be much higher than the village) you can normally ski from mid-December to early April but with low resorts (height less than 800m and skiing no higher than 2500m) this could be mid-January to mid-March only. Higher resorts with glacier skiing have the longer skiing seasons.

In recent years the coming of snow has been unreliable so many resorts have invested in 'artificial snow' to supplement what nature doesn't bring – water is sprayed onto the slopes at high pressure and under cold temperatures so that it freezes and creates snow. Where there are these facilities you don't have to choose such a high resort as long as it is cold enough for these 'snow cannons' to produce snow. Artificial snow is not as forgiving as natural snow and can be much more slippery so you should be careful.

Dates

Those lucky enough not to be restricted by their children's school holidays, work or personal commitments, can choose the best time for their chosen resort. However if you are limited to early or late in the season a high resort with a good snow record must be chosen. If the holiday must be in 'high season' choose a resort that is not likely to be too congested: crowds and queues quickly develop if every skier in the village has to use its one lift to the slopes every morning.

In the notes on countries offering ski resorts, we have used the following coding:

a – ski school   c – Good adult après ski
b – family resort   d – Good facilities for non-skiers

What resort flavour would suit you?

Little or large, old or new, high or low? There is no 'perfect' resort, the choice will probably be a compromise of different priorities.

The pretty, traditional resorts look wonderful in pictures, but most were not built as ski resorts so bear in mind that the slopes could be a walk (or even a bus ride) from your accommodation. The local life and village character can more than make up for some inconvenience though.

How do you find out about a resort? This book is too small to act as a resort guide but they can be obtained from book shops, and allow you to do a lot of research yourself. If it all seems too complicated the Ski Club of Great Britain provides its members with a Resort Information service and it also keeps records of the snow conditions over the years.

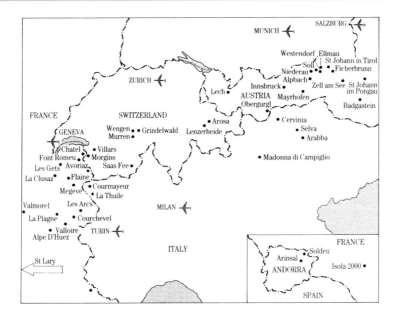

Andorra?

In the Pyreneean mountains between France and Spain lies the duty-free principality of Andorra. In this small country the ski areas are particularly suited to beginners. Living costs are low and the fun factor high. In addition the ski schools attract many English speaking ski instructors – a great help to Britons learning a new sport. The following resorts have particularly good runs for beginners: Arinsal *a; Soldeu *a.

Austria?

More than half of the beginners going skiing choose the smaller, traditional ski villages of Austria, attracted by the character of the villages and the friendly welcome. Many are farming communities which have developed into ski areas and are not as high as purpose built ski resorts. If you are planning to take an early or late season skiing holiday, you should check the heights of such resorts. As a beginner, try one of these places: Alpbach; Badgastein *cd; Ellmau; Fieberbrunn; Innsbruck (as a base for other resorts) *cd; Lech; Mayrhofen *acd; Niederau *ab; Obergurgl; St Johann im Pongau; St Johann in Tirol *acd; Soll *ac; Westendorf; Zell am

France?

France is well known for its modern resorts built at high altitudes where accommodation is in small apartments or characterless hotels, all perched conveniently on the slopes. For the sake of this convenience, the absence of an onion-domed church and pretty, cobbled streets is a small sacrifice to make to save having to stagger in ski boots to the lifts – often armed with two pairs of children's skis! However, this resort type is certainly not the rule; some of the modern resorts have been carefully planned with style and character, and there are many old towns that have become ski centres. Try: Alpe d'Huez *b; Avoriaz; Chatel; Courchevel; Flaine *ab; Font Romeu; Isola 2000; La Clusaz *bc; La Plagne *b; Les Arcs *ab; Les Gets *d; Megeve *cd; St Lary; Valmorel *b; Valloire.

Italy?

If your tummy speaks loudest and finances are tight Italian pasta and good wine will be the lure of Italy. Resorts in Italy tend to divide into two categories. Those of alpine style which share mountains on the border of France or Switzerland, and those in a range called the Dolomites which runs generally east-west into south eastern Austria. The Dolomites are near vertical rock formations, stretching up from sloping bases on which the skiing takes place. As a rule the skiing is easy and surrounded by spectacular scenery. Due to their proximity to Austria these villages are very Austrian in flavour. Try: Arabba; Cervinia; Courmayeur *ac; La Thuile; Madonna di Campiglio; Marileva; Selva *cd.

Switzerland?

Swiss resorts are efficient, clean, honest and, due to building restrictions, unspoilt by ugly buildings. Depending on the region French, German or Italian may be spoken. The reputation that this country is expensive is true, but visitors can be sure of good value. Try: Arosa *acd; Grindelwald; Lenzerheide *d; Morgins; Murren *abd; Saas Fee; Villars *ad; Wengen *a.

or even Scotland?

It should not be forgotten that the Scottish ski areas can provide excellent skiing – when the weather is good, particularly since weather conditions vary and for those who live in the south the prospect of travelling up to Scotland is almost inconceivable. Since conditions vary flexibility is needed. Those who live in the north should consider trying out our native slopes. Information on each area can be found from the Scottish National Tourist Office and on snow conditions by dialling 0898 654 654. You can be sure that English will be spoken!

Getting it all booked up

Once you have decided where to go the decisions become easier. Simply how to get there, and what accommodation you want to have when you get there. What could be simpler? Although you can organise your own accommodation and transport, as a raw beginner to the sport you could end up making expensive mistakes through inexperience. Leave it up to those who know how, the tour operators. And as long as you choose a reputable tour operator and you have selected your resort carefully, all arrangements should now be made for you with practised efficiency.

Tour operators

Most travel agents now stock the brochures from the larger tour operators, but there are many more and the biggest is not always the best. There are over 200 ski tour operators to choose from offering a choice of different resorts and packages. In most instances it would be advisable to get some unbiased advice about the resort then talk to the operator direct about the package they are selling. Obtain details from a selection of different operators offering the same resort for price comparisons. Many operators offer incentives such as group discounts or children at reduced rates.

With the growth of the skiing market operators have begun to offer beginners weeks, or 'Learn to Ski' weeks which often include ski school, ski pass and equipment hire. Not only do they mean that you will be among like-minded, like-ability people, they are often very good value. However, as long as you choose a resort that is suitable for beginners you don't have to go on a special 'Learn To Ski Week' to find your ski legs, particularly since most operators will have Representatives to help you sort yourself out.

Travelling out

Ski clothes are bulky, and you will therefore have rather cumbersome luggage to carry. But however bulky they are, try to avoid wearing your snow boots because your feet will soon become unbearably hot and smelly on the journey. Keep them near the surface of your packing, though, in case they are needed for wading through snow on arrival in the resort.

The easiest way to travel is to fly from one of the many airports in Britain that handle departures to ski countries. At weekends during high season the airports will be crowded with skiers, and you could well find yourself wishing you had walked. If you decide to fly look at the transfer time from the airport to the resort – it could be anything from half an hour to six hours from the airport – resorts with long transfers are difficult with young children. Take some local currency for stops on the way and a picnic.

Many resorts, particularly in France and Switzerland, are well served with rail links. Although rail travel from Britain is quite expensive it is very relaxing and there is nothing more wonderful than waking up to snowy mountains having left Britain behind in rain.

Road travel is the final option. Either go in a coach (usually sleeping uncomfortably over night), or drive yourself. The latter can be tiring and if you undertake this your car must be correctly serviced to cope with the long journey and cold. Check all the requirements for foreign driving and the use of motorways; in some countries it is obligatory to carry snow chains. Going by car is financially viable for two or more people and certainly gives more flexibility in the resort. A word of warning: take snow chains, a shovel and be prepared to dig the car out after a night's snowfall. Coach travel is usually cheaper than driving yourself.

The accommodation

There are three alternatives each with advantages.

Increasing in popularity is the British idea of a 'home' in the resort, that is a 'chalet party'. A house, or part of a house, is rented by the tour operator and staffed by British staff. Friends can either book the whole chalet, or individuals can join a group. Meals are provided in the chalet, you can come and go when you want to without upsetting others and entertain guests to tea!. There are many advantages to a chalet party in social terms; creature comforts sometimes suffer from shortages of showers, however, (baths are rare) and hot water may be limited when twelve people want to use it before dinner.

For an absolute holiday choose a hotel. These range from small family run pensions to large and luxurious buildings. Bed & Breakfast in a hotel gives you the chance to try out local restaurants, but budget carefully! Those taking full board (including lunch) will find it restrictive having to return to the hotel for lunch (unless the hotel is right on the slopes). For most half board is the best option.

The budget skier, or those who want complete privacy should choose to self cater. Accommodation ranges from renting your own chalet down to apartments (large and small, although more often very small). While self catering gives flexibility, you should be aware that shopping after skiing, cooking and washing up after each meal soon begins to become tedious and the temptation to go out for meals becomes overwhelming, obliterating your careful budget! Those who travel by car can to some extent bring food, but foreign food shops always make the idea of adventurous cooking much more appealing! Beware, unless carefully managed a self catering holiday could become more expensive than you bargained for.

Check your insurance

Normal holiday insurance is not sufficient for a skiing holiday. Skiing is considered a risk sport and if you do not take out a specific skiing insurance claims will be invalid. Even if you do have a winter sports policy check it carefully for exclusions before you decide to do something different like hang gliding, tobogganing, or even ski racing. Remember, also, that this is a 'holiday' insurance and only covers you for incidents during your holiday time and no treatment back at home. As with any insurance, if you are going to claim, keep any receipts.

Many ski tour operators include insurance in the package. If this is the case you should obtain a full written description of what is included. There are specialist companies that sell winter sports insurance packages separately (Douglas Cox Tyrie on 081 534 9595 is one such) and the Ski Club of Great Britain can advise on the minimum you should be covered for.

If you are not satisfied with the amount of cover that your tour operator gives, or insurance is not included with your holiday, find a policy. Insurance is an area which should not be economised on. You can be sure that the more cover your policy has the higher the costs of the premium will be.

Which ever insurance you have make sure that you take with you the details of the policy, the name and telephone number of the insurance company and their loss adjuster so that you can prove you are insured if you suddenly need to. Some companies issue a card to carry with you.

You should be covered for . . .

Policies vary, but at the very minimum yours should include:

Medical, rescue, repatriation – transporting you from the place of accident, treating you, then getting you home.

Personal liability (Third Party) – if you cause damage to somebody else who as a result incurs medical expenses, misfortune and unemployment, you will be liable for their costs.

Additionally, you will want to be sure that you are covered for *loss/theft* of your *baggage, skis* (plus hired equipment), *money* and *skipass*. Most packages will include *holiday cancellation* as long as you cancel for one of the reasons listed in the certificate of insurance – check before cancelling! It is for this reason that you would be well advised to take out insurance as soon as you have booked your holiday in case, for example, you have to cancel due to being summoned for jury service or are too ill to go.

Many ski policies include sums payable as compensation for misery if you have *delayed departure, interrupted travel, missed departure* or *no snow* (payment for the latter is very specific). *Personal Accident* is a surprising item which is usually included; it means that you will be compensated if, as the result of an accident, you are permanently disabled. You would then receive a lump sum (if you die your executors receive the sum), usually an amount from £5,000–£20,000 – not worth having an accident for!

The sum of cover for each of the above items will vary with different policies, and will rise each year, so take time to shop around – expect to pay about £25 for a week.

If you are skiing in EEC countries the DHSS Euroform E111 covers some medical expenses incurred in EEC countries but only the very basics and it does not include mountain rescue, repatriation, ambulance or private treatment and other ski related items that you will want. It must be supplemented.

You may also come across the 'Carte Neige' which covers you for mountain rescue and limited medical costs in Europe. Some tour operators use Carte Neige but incorporate additional items to the basic policy with a British insurance broker.

SKI CLOTHING

Now that you have decided to head for the slopes your next concern will be your new clothing. The choice should not be made lightly; remember practicality far outweighs fashion and being 'cool' (you will find wearing jeans very cool!). It is essential to be well clothed; mountain weather is so variable that you must be able to cope with extremes of temperature and high winds, as well as warm sunny weather. Layers are easily added and taken away, and keep you warmer than the bulk of one big jumper.

As a beginner you will inevitably fall in the snow and frequently find yourself standing still during classes. It is essential to be warm and waterproof which is why you must wear specialist clothing.

Hire or buy?

You will soon discover that skiing is a compulsively expensive sport. Once you are hooked you won't be able to limit yourself to the cost of a week's holiday, whatever level you attain. There are always accessories to add, colours to coordinate and technical advances to keep abreast with. A raw beginner will be considering whether to hire or buy a skisuit, whilst the committed show-off agonises over whether to be seen on the slopes in last season's fashions, using skis from the season before.

First time skiers often become addicted to the sport no matter what the costs are. You will find owning your own clothing preferable to hiring, firstly because the number of rental outlets is limited and secondly because skiing jackets have become fashion garments which can be worn back at home. If you are prepared to pay for a garment you will not regret the initial outlay.

Hiring is particularly recommended for growing children, however. Skiworld (071 602 4820) and all but the London branch of Ellis Brigham rent clothing, the latter doing a roaring trade in the schools category as well as operating a regular mail order service. Some tour operators will also offer a ski clothing rental package for children as part of the holiday.

Budget ski wear

Countrywide chains which sell good value ski wear are: C&A, M&S, Boots (selected branches), Next, Champion Sports, Astral Sports, Ellis Brigham, Wilderness Ways (North of England), Nevisport (Scotland), Snow & Rock and selected Olympus Sports outlets. Specialist ski shops often offer more choice at the upper end of the market, where for a little more investment you can obtain greater style and better fabrics. With the popularity of skiing you will probably find that you have friends who ski from whom you can borrow some items. Don't be persuaded to borrow boots, which must be an *exact* fit – they will ruin your holiday if they aren't.

The outer layer

Although one pieces look smart and prevent snow getting in at your midriff, novices are better off buying inexpensive salopettes (padded ski trousers cut high like dungarees) and a jacket which can be worn in the evenings, too. The jacket should be roomy enough for a few shirts and a sweater under it and should not ride up at the waist. Combined with a pair of ski pants it should completely protect the waist area. The salopettes should give a good fit over the tops of boots to prevent snow entering.

When buying clothing you will notice that the fabrics have differing properties, some of which make garments very expensive but ensure extra protection. Look out for the names: Gore-Tex, Entrant, Super Microft, Tactel and Super Exceltech (all waterproof/breathable fabrics); Cyclone (insulation and waterproof/breathable); Thinsulate, Hollowfil and Isodry (insulation/warmth).

However much you pay for a ski outfit, read the washing instructions carefully. Some can only be dry cleaned which is costly and never seems to work as well as washing. Others have to be washed gently at low temperatures and often by hand. Waterproofing materials such as Gore-Tex and Entrant must not be spin-dried and need to be double rinsed or they may lose their special properties.

Accessories

Unfortunately, it doesn't just stop with a skisuit. There are other essential accessories to consider. To begin with, what should you wear underneath it?

Unless you have splashed out on an expensive functional outfit (one which is well insulated and waterproofed, see above) you will probably need a thermal long-sleeved vest and long johns which are worn underneath light layers such as a polo neck and sweatshirt or sweater, rather than a thick jumper. Many people prefer natural fibres like silk (expensive) and cotton. The newer man-made thermal materials are also comfortable to wear and remove moisture from the skin. Layers are better than bulk.

You will need special ski gloves or mitts to keep your hands warm and protect them from cuts when falling on hard snow. Wool gloves are no good, they get wet and cold. Mitts are warmer than gloves but cumbersome; you may have to remove them to fiddle with your boot clips and zips. Make sure that the cuff of the glove bridges the gap between glove and sleeve. It is a good idea to have thin inner gloves for cold days. Skimping when buying gloves is a false economy and can lead to misery on the slopes. Get good quality ones; they'll last for years.

The body loses most of its heat through the head so a hat (or headband to keep the ears cosy) is essential. If you are going to a high resort in January take a balaclava, or a neck roll which can be pulled up to protect the face.

Socks should be long enough to go higher than the boot. Modern ski boots are now well insulated and so thick knitted socks are not needed. A thin, well fitting pair gives the best comfort particularly the loopstitch tube-style type. Ribbed or knitted ones may chafe.

Bare essentials

Sunshine is a serious threat and even on a dull day in the mountains ultra violet rays come through the cloud layer – to say nothing of their reflection from the snow.

Use a high sun protection factor (SPF) cream and lipsalve. Start, with a minimum of factor 15 especially for sensitive skins and children. Those by Elizabeth Arden go as high as 34. You should take the tube with you on the slopes and top up often; try Piz Buin and Ambre Solaire in minitubes for convenience. Look out for waterproof ones so you don't need to reapply every time you nose dive onto the snow. And don't forget your lips.

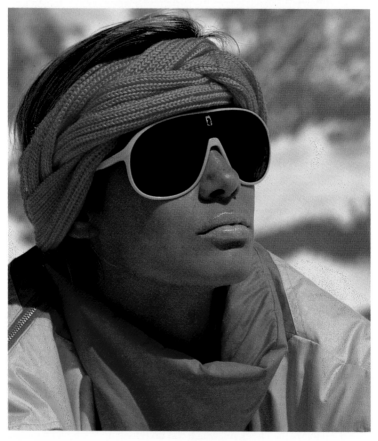

The sunglasses that you use at home will be unlikely to give the correct eye protection required for snowy conditions. Even if it is not particularly sunny there will be a steady glare from the snow which in large amounts will cause painful eyes and could lead to snow blindness. Again, when buying skiing glasses and goggles do not economise (always take both with you – mountain weather is unpredictable and goggles are warmer in bad weather). Buy ones with a UV filter (Bollé, Vuarnet, Ray-Ban, Carrera, Uvex, Alpina, Smith and Scott are good). Glasses with side pieces keep out the glare better but guarantee 'owl eyes' in a tanned face.

Equipment

Skiing 'hardwear' (boots, skis, bindings and poles) is expensive. Always hire this for your first trip since, as a beginner, you will not know what to buy and as you improve your requirements will change, plus there is the faint possibility that you will not take to skiing. When you later decide to buy equipment take good advice. The Ski Club of Great Britain offers its members an Equipment Advisory Service.

Boots

There are two different styles of boot. The rear entry where the back of the boot opens to let the foot in then clips shut, and the front entry which fastens with a row of adjustable clips down the front, like a conventional lace up shoe. Each has a variety of adjustments to alter the exact fit but you are more likely to find the former, simpler version for hire.

Most skiers remember the misery of painful feet in ill-fitting hire boots tried on in a hurry. When trying on the boot take a well-fitting sock to the shop then walk about and make sure that the fit is comfortable but not too sloppy, and that you can wiggle your toes easily. By all means try on more than one pair and more than one model. If the one you take feels uncomfortable when skiing, go back to the shop and swap it – even if it is half way through the day. Don't grin and bear it. Your feet and legs may be too sore to ski the next day.

Fastening the boots too tightly (in a desperate attempt to feel more in control) will cut blood supply or press on sensitive nerves and cause a lot of pain. On the other hand padding out with lots of socks doesn't help either; if you do have odd shaped feet and have persistent rubbing put some 'second skin' or thin tape on the affected region at the beginning of each day.

Boots will be the first item of ski 'hardwear' that you decide to buy. When doing so be honest with the shop assistant about your standard – don't go for the racing model (yet!). Most first time buyers go for a size too big, wanting them to feel 'comfy'. This is a mistake, you sacrifice control of the skis. Try on the smallest pair that feels comfortable because in a ski shop your feet will tend to be hot and bigger, and boots always seem to stretch (the inner material packs down). If you can obtain a 'comfort guarantee' so much the better. This means that the shop will accept the boots back in exchange or for credit, less a hire charge, if you find them uncomfortable. It is best to buy boots in Britain if you are uncertain unless you see a bargain abroad.

Skis

The type of ski that you use will depend on your weight, height and skiing ability. As a beginner you should always hire skis and let the technician decide your correct size. As your standard improves the ski length that you can handle will increase. Even if you are a beginner you should not be fobbed off with skis in a bad condition. Look for deep gouges in the sole or heavy nicks in the metal edges (these should be sharp to help control). If you are unhappy about the skis you are offered, be firm about having another pair. If you find your hire skis exceptionally difficult to control you could ask to swap them for a shorter pair for the first few days.

Later on when you get better you may decide to buy skis. As with boots, do not buy more advanced, stiffer, longer skis thinking that they will last you longer. It will be difficult to control them and your confidence will be wrecked. Essentially a ski is as good as the skier (although certain models are designed to handle different conditions better than others) – invest in good skiing instruction first before buying an advanced ski.

Bindings

The bindings are designed to hold your boots on to your skis firmly enough for normal skiing and loosely enough to release the boot if you fall awkwardly. Modern bindings are very safety conscious and the release setting is calculated on an internationally agreed scale known as the DIN setting. The ski technician will ask for your weight and level of ski ability to help him select the correct DIN setting for you.

If you are buying a binding, look for one to suit your ability. The DIN setting you require should come at about the mid point of the range of settings on that binding.

All modern bindings are fitted with ski brakes to prevent the ski running away downhill when it comes off your boot, so don't worry about losing the ski in a fall. It is more important to ensure that it *does* come off.

Before putting your foot into a ski binding when on the slopes, bang your boot with the ski pole to knock off any snow stuck to the sole. In this way you can ensure that your boot fits cleanly into the bindings.

Ski Poles

As a beginner your poles will be used mainly for balance, so don't choose a flashy curved downhill model which will only trip you up (even if they do match your skisuit!). When you hire skis, the poles are usually included in the package. To choose the right length of pole, hold it under the basket and, with the handle touching the ground, your forearm should be horizontal. It is a good idea to try out the various types of hand grip with your ski gloves on, to find the most comfortable arrangement for you.

Hiring your equipment

Hiring has its advantages and disadvantages. The disadvantages are that you cannot be sure of the quality of equipment you will get and each time you go skiing you will have to spend time in a ski shop hiring again. However, anyone going at the beginning of the season usually gets new equipment unless there is little snow in the resort when the shop will only let out 'rock-hoppers'. You can imagine what this implies about the soles of the skis! As a beginner you should hire all 'hardwear', however, and so you need only consider whether to hire your gear at home or in the resort.

Hiring in the resort can waste valuable skiing time queuing in a shop where the assistant might not speak English well and will be too busy perhaps to fit you properly. The great advantage is that you can go back as often as you need to change unsuitable equipment, and you should. Some ski tour operators will offer ski hire packages with the holiday in which case the rep will certainly be in the shop on day one. These packages normally represent a discount on the hire price.

Most resort hire shops have a price list for different categories of ski, and if you are prepared to pay a little more, you can hire anything from the newest recreational beginner ski up to the latest racing model (if you are up to it). Better still, if you are thinking of buying skis, you can hire a different pair every day to try out the models that interest you most.

It is cheaper to hire in the UK. Some ski shops rent 'hardwear' and most are small outlets rather than chains. The range offered for hire may vary from limited to wide, and you will have the hassle of carting extra luggage to and fro.

A company called Airport Skis offer a viable compromise covering the above pros and cons. They now have eight outlets: Gatwick (including the North Terminal), Hayes (for Heathrow), Manchester (Airport and Blacks ski shop), London (Moss Bros, Blacks in Holborn and the Ski Club of Great Britain as a collection and drop off point), Dover Harbour (for self-drive, where you can hire roof rack and snow chains too) and Basildon (Magic Mountain). You can select equipment in one and pick up or drop off at another. Remember to leave home early enough to allow adequate selection time. There is a guarantee that if your equipment is unsatisfactory for any reason and you have to hire something else in the resort you will be reimbursed the resort shop's hire fee (on presentation of receipt).

Final tip

When out in the resort, all hire skis look perplexingly similar. Try to recognise which are yours – fix on an identifying feature – and remember exactly where you last left them!

Ski checklist

This suggested list will help you remember to take all that might be needed on your ski trip. Add other more personal requirements to the list yourself.

☐ SKIS

☐ BOOTS

☐ POLES

☐ SKI SUIT/JACKET & TROUSERS

☐ SKI/POLO SHIRT

☐ SOCKS

☐ HAT/HEAD BAND/NECK ROLL

☐ BUMBAG/BACKPACK

☐ COTTON HANDKERCHIEF

☐ LIFT PASS HOLDER

☐ APRÈS SKI CLOTHING

☐ MINOR FIRST AID KIT

☐ SEWING KIT

☐ CONTINENTAL ADAPTER

☐ READING BOOKS/GAMES

☐ TRAVEL DOCUMENTS

☐ INSURANCE DETAILS

☐ TRAVELLERS CHEQUES/
EUROCHEQUES/CREDIT CARD

☐ SKI BAG

☐ BOOT BAG

☐ SKI REPAIR KIT

☐ THIN JUMPER/SWEATSHIRT

☐ THERMAL UNDERWEAR

☐ GLOVES/MITTENS

☐ SUNCREAM & LIPSALVE

☐ SMALL PURSE (FOR ON
SLOPES)

☐ SWIMSUIT/SPORTS CLOTHES

☐ PHOTO FOR LIFTPASS

☐ APRÈS SKI BOOTS

☐ CAMERA AND SPARE FILM

☐ ALARM CLOCK

☐ HAIRDRYER/RAZOR

☐ FOREIGN DICTIONARY

☐ PASSPORT

☐ FOREIGN CASH

GETTING FIT

It is never too soon to start preparing your body for skiing. Ideally you should aim to maintain a good level of year-round fitness and step up your training with exercises specific to skiing prior to your departure.

Why should I make the effort?

Fitness increases your enjoyment of any activity and this is especially true of skiing, which is very tiring at the beginner level. There's lots of falling down, getting up and climbing back up the nursery slope. As a novice you tend to fight gravity instead of allowing it to work for you. Add to this hard work an occasional feeling of fear and constant muscular tension and imagine how an unfit person is going to feel at the end of the day. A fit body can cope with these stresses without exhaustion setting in.

Subjecting muscles suddenly to strenuous exercise and movements to which they are unused will result in stiffness and pain for the following day or two. This will certainly affect both your enjoyment and progress. Avoid this situation by strengthening those muscles.

Finally, fitness can help avoid injury. For example, strong leg muscles will protect the knee joint, which is very vulnerable in skiing. Similarly, a flexible body can cope better with awkward falls, preventing soft tissue tears and strains.

How can I get fit?

Broadly speaking physical fitness falls into three categories:
cardio-respiratory
muscular strength and endurance
flexibility.

All three types of fitness are necessary for skiing.

Cardio-respiratory (heart-lungs) fitness is sometimes referred to as aerobic capacity or stamina. It reduces your tendency to get out of breath and protects you against the feeling that you might have a heart attack! Extra stamina will enable you to keep going longer – skiing and nightlife – without becoming fatigued.

Muscular strength is needed to push yourself up from a fall, whereas **endurance** is required when the body has to repeat the same movements over and over again – such as those required to make skis turn – or to maintain the correct ski stance.

Flexibility (stretching) is important to enable you to attain correct posture and in preventing torn muscle and tendons.

Exercises

Please note: this is not a complete workout but simply some suggestions for exercises for skiers.

Aerobic

Cycling is perfect because it uses the legs in a similar way to skiing. Running (if you are unfit start with brisk walking or jogging) and swimming are alternatives.

Muscle Work

The front of the thigh is used a lot in skiing and strengthening this area supports the knee. Sit on a table with the edge behind your knees. Support your weight on your hands. Slowly extend one leg until it is fully straightened, hold for two seconds and lower as far back as possible. Do as many repetitions as you can (start with ten) then work the other leg. Do as many sets of ten as possible, and increase the number as you get fitter.

Beginners start skiing using a movement called the Snowplough. This requires strong outer thighs and buttocks. Lie on your side in a straight line. One hand supports the shoulder, the other arm is placed on the floor taking the weight of the body. Bend the lower leg for support. Ensure that your upper hip is pushed forward. Flex the foot of the upper leg, tense the muscles and with the toe pointing slightly down, raise and lower slowly ensuring the knee faces forward. Repeat as above.

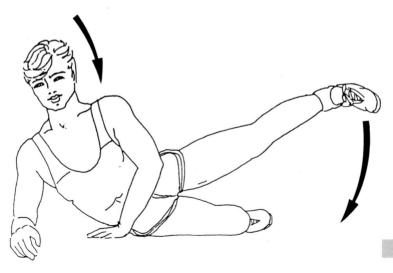

A strong abdomen is needed to maintain the pelvic tilt position vital to the basic skiing stance. It also looks attractive in tight skisuits! Lie on your back, knees bent at right angles feet about shoulder distance apart. Push your lower back into the floor, tucking your bottom under and tensing the buttocks slightly. Place your hands on your thighs, chin towards chest and slowly curl your upper body up, sliding hands towards knees. If you can, cup your knees with your hands and hold for two seconds before slowly lowering. Repeat as above.

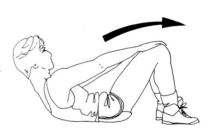

Beginners do spend an inordinate amount of time struggling to get up after a tumble. Lots of muscles are involved in this struggle, but the ones in the upper back are probably most important. The following exercise will help. With ankles and knees flexed (feet about hip distance apart) bend forward until your upper body is nearly parallel to the floor, back flat. Extend your arms down with fingers spread, then make fists and pull them up towards your armpits, keeping the upper arm squeezed inwards. Do this slowly and with control. Repeat as above.

Flexibility

For many skiers ankle flexibility is vital to technique, but difficult to achieve. This can be due to tight calf muscles and Achilles tendons. Try the following exercise. Stand leaning against a wall with one leg bent and the other straight as far back as possible with the heel down. Both toes point forward. Tuck your bottom under and keep hips aligned, pushing them forward. Hold the stretch for at least ten seconds then stretch the other leg. Now do the same thing with the weight back a little and the rear leg bent. You should feel the stretch lower down in the Achilles tendon. Women who wear high heels get bunched calf muscles and should pay special attention to flexibility.

Lots of skiers, particularly beginners, tend to allow their backs to arch and bottom to stick out. A flexible lower back will help you attain the correct skiing posture. Lie on your back and bring your knees towards your chest. Hold behind the thighs and ease knees to armpits, allowing the buttocks to come off the floor slightly. Hold for as long as feels comfortable.

As the front of the thigh gets a battering when skiing, stretch it out well. Holding something for support, bend one foot towards the buttock, take hold of the ankle (not toe) and ease it in. Line up your thighs, tuck the bottom under, don't arch your back. Hold for ten seconds and repeat on the other leg.

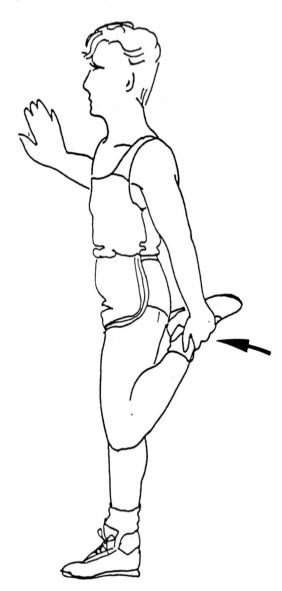

When should I start the exercises?

Start stepping up your existing routine at least six weeks before you leave. Aerobic exercises should be done continuously for a minimum of 20 minutes three times a week, on alternate days. Add to this programme a further 15 or more minutes of specific muscle training. It is safe to stretch every day; in fact the more time you spend on improving your flexibility the better.

If you are unused to exercise don't go mad. Start with less and build it up. For example start with one exercise repeated ten times in strength work, then go on to do two or three sets of ten, after which you can add repetitions working up to, say three sets of 20 repetitions. Or start with ten minutes aerobic exercise building it up in length and frequency until you can do 30 minutes every other day. You can also increase exercise intensity in strength work by adding wrist or ankle weights (make your own by filling a length of stocking with lentils and tying it round your ankle or hold a can of baked beans!

Where should I exercise?

You can exercise at home but there is little incentive to keep going if you are on your own. There are aids to exercise: mini-trampolines (rebounders), dumbells, skipping ropes and machines designed for skiers which might help to keep your interest on the job in hand.

If you find going out to a get-fit session is more motivating then join a pre-ski class. Contact your local education authority or YMCA to find out where they are in your area. Better still join a club which offers exercise classes and a gym with all the modern machinery. Some clubs even have swimming pools.

Remember to wear correct footwear – well-cushioned sports shoes if you are running or attending an aerobics class. Comfortable clothing that you can move in is vital. Wear layers that you can remove if you get overheated.

Dry slopes

The best exercise for skiing is skiing. As soon as you feel fit why not book a course of lessons on your local dry slope (send a large SAE and 50p to the Ski Club of Great Britain, 118 Eaton Square, London SW1W 9AF for a list). You will learn all the basics: how to put on equipment, balance, basic stance, falling down and getting up, right up to snowplough turns. This will save precious time on your holiday.

WHEN YOU ARRIVE IN THE RESORT

At the end of your first day you'll know that all the worry was worth it and all the preparation paid off. Collapsed in an arm chair, exhausted limbs at last allowed to relax, you will start to feel 'normal' once again. Dining in a restaurant, having a glass of local wine in your hand and a fork of meat in the bubbling fondu pot, is all part of celebrating your achievement of skiing a near horizontal slope without falling!

Ready for the slopes? You will need:

Ski equipment

Your first port of call on day one will be the hire shop. Most shops that sell equipment also hire it and your tour operator representative will recommend one. If you travelled independently and don't have a recommendation go to the nearest shop to your accommodation or one that gives a discount; you may have to leave a deposit or credit card enprint. Once you've got your kit note down what your equipment looks like so that you don't lose it.

The ski shop will show you how to put on your boots and clip them up, and how to get in and out of the bindings. Ask them to show you the correct way to hold your poles and straps.

Other belongings

Each day be sure to take out **gloves**, **glasses**, **suncream**, **money** (cash and credit card), **handkerchief**, **warm hat**, **insurance details** and **lift pass**. It is a good idea to try and remember a silly rhyme that reminds you to take everything out each day – you may need a bumbag or small back pack to carry things in. If you need to go to the bank be aware that banking hours vary, but are often during skiing time.

Lift pass

Some lifts for beginners are free but most have to be paid for in advance – you buy a pass which has to be shown to allow use of the lifts. As a beginner, buy the one that covers the smallest area; your ski instructor or tour operator rep will advise you on which lifts you will need to use. You won't be using all of them on the first day but if you want to explore more slopes the pass can be changed to cover a larger area if you pay the difference. Tour operators often buy the passes in advance for you, having talked to you about your needs. This discussion may take place during your airport to resort transfer journey, so that passes can be organised as soon as you arrive.

Passes can be bought from either the Tourist Office in the town centre or at the bottom of the main lift. Some passes require a photograph and have to be shown regularly or punched, or passed through a computer so it helps to have it permanently accessible. Take a passport sized picture with you to save having to go and get one done in the resort. Keep your pass tied to you because once lost replacement is difficult (often impossible).

Ski map

The runs available in a resort are displayed on a ski map. Admittedly, it is difficult to get your bearings at first when skiing, particularly in cloudy weather if the visibility is poor. Ski maps are free and can be picked up at the bottom of major lifts, in restaurants and about the resort. Always carry one with you.

By studying the map carefully you will get an idea of where you are going – it is easy to just follow your instructor, ignorant of the route, but it is much more fun to know where you are and take a part in the route planning. Plus it could be helpful if you get lost or want to meet people. From the map you can tell what type of route leads down, what type of lift goes up and where the mountain restaurants are!

Ski school

All beginners should enrol for ski school. To confuse you, in some French resorts there may be a choice of two schools, one part of the national system, and another set up in rivalry which may aim to be better in a specific area. You will have to ask the locals to recommend one. Go to the ski school office and explain that you want an English speaking instructor and have never skied before. If you are above beginner level, having skied on a dry slope, you may have to do a test to see which class to join. Whatever your standard you should protest if the class is larger than twelve people because it will mean less individual attention for you and more standing around getting cold and bored.

It is recommended to join for a complete week of morning classes at least; add afternoons if you don't feel too tired. As well as being a way to get onto the slopes quickly (classes have priority in lift queues), ski school is a fun way to meet other people and find out a bit more about the area from your instructor.

Classes normally start at 9.00 a.m. and last for two or three hours. The afternoon classes usually run from 2.00 to 4.00 p.m. If you want to do the whole day the instructor will explain where to meet in the afternoon. At the end of the week you can take a test if you wish, which will be useful the following year for explaining to your next instructor what standard you have reached.

Let's get moving

A few tips:

1 Drink plenty of water, bottled if the tap water isn't safe, to counteract the effects of altitude, notably dehydration, which drains muscle energy.

2 If you are taking instruction insist on a teacher who speaks good English. If you are not satisfied with the instructor's English then ask for a change – gone are the days of accepting 'bend ze knees' and 'follow me'. Some European ski schools now employ B.A.S.I. (British Association of Ski Instructors) trained instructors who have a reputation of being amongst the best teachers in the world.

3 Remember when carrying skis over your shoulder, to keep the tips (sharp end) forward leaving the tails behind you. (See photo). Look out for people around you; no-one likes getting hit by a pair of skis, and you don't want to spend your first week in a law suit rather than a ski suit

Hold your ski poles in your other hand and use them like a walking stick for balance, especially if the road is a bit slippery.

You arrive at the beginners' area, and, after loosening the skiing muscles and getting the circulation going, tighten your boots and put your skis on.

When walking on skis don't lift them off the ground, simply slide them forward alternately, using your poles for balance.

As your left foot slides forward bring your right hand forward and plant your pole firmly in the snow opposite your left boot; this should give you support to push your right foot forwards. Bring your left hand forward, plant your pole and repeat.

This sounds fairly complicated, but when you're on skis it will seem quite straightforward, and it really is worth cultivating your co-ordination right from the start – it is so important later on.

Turning around

To change direction make small steps to your right or left, making sure your skis don't cross – lift the tips slightly to make these steps, and use your poles for support.

Sliding

On the way back to your starting area try standing equally on both feet and pushing yourself forward using both poles. Begin the push with your poles almost vertical in the snow beside your feet. Push off both poles simultaneously and then bring your arms forward ready for the next push. You are now moving on skis. It feels great!

There are other exercises you can do on the flat, to get used to having six feet long 'feet'. Try side stepping; this will come in useful when you want to gain height up a slope.

Start by lifting the right ski and stepping it out about a foot to the side; as you place it on the snow plant both poles for balance, now lift your left ski to join the right one. Stand on the left ski and step out again with the right one and so on.

Try to get a rhythm going by humming something. 'Humpty Dumpty' works well; and don't forget to practise this in both directions. Now some theory:

Understand how your skis work

Skiing is all about turning. We turn for enjoyment, to avoid obstacles and people, to control our speed, to get from one place to another or in some cases, to win a race. The tracks we leave down a mountain can tell the type of person we are and how we feel on a given day. Short aggressive turns or long and easy going turns can say a lot about us and how we like to ski. However the one thing common to both the World Cup racer and the beginner is they both need to turn. Now let us look at how to achieve this, through the equipment that helps us turn. The ski, the design of which has been with us for about 5000 years, is a turning tool; when used properly it can be a highly efficient means of carrying you down a mountain. The second half of this book aims to give you a basic understanding of the principles of skiing and so can be followed alone or used to complement any lessons you may take.

To help understand the ski we will look at how it is designed. Let's look at a ski from two angles; firstly, as it sits flat on the ground from the side and secondly looking straight down on it from above.

You will see it touches the ground at the tip (sharp end) and the tail (blunt end), and does not touch in the middle – this is called 'Positive Camber'

and like all the other parameters of ski design, will vary from ski to ski. The ski is flexible and when you stand on it, it will flatten under your

weight and touch the ground in the middle. Imagine putting a block of wood under the tip and tail and standing on it; the ski will flex further, into

'Reverse Camber'. If you were then to bounce up and down slightly you would feel the flexibility and camber of the ski. This is the way the ski acts over the undulating surface of the snow, helping to maintain ski/snow contact.

Now look down on the ski from above. You should notice, although not as obvious as camber, that the ski is wider at the tip and tail than in the middle. This factor is called 'sidecut', or 'waisting' and like camber will vary from ski to ski. In a slalom ski the sidecut is more pronounced than in a giant slalom or downhill ski.

Now let us look at combining these two properties. When you put a moving ski on its edge in snow and press on it, it will make an arc in the snow. More pressure gives a smaller tighter arc or turn and less pressure gives a longer arc or turn.

Ian pressing hard on one ski to show what reverse camber looks like close up.

When hiring or buying skis as a beginner the shop technician will advise you about length and type. However, as a general guide beginners' skis should be about head height or slightly below, depending on your weight and fitness and should be an easy turning 'all round' ski.

Understand how your ski boots work

Ski boots are made of synthetic materials, and give various performance levels from beginner to racer. As a beginner you should look for a boot from the beginning to the middle of the range available. It is no use buying the top racing boot (with all the go faster features), as it has been designed for the aggressive advanced skier, and will be stiff which may impede your progress. Your boot must be flexible in a forward direction and yet give you support in a lateral or sideways direction. This is important to allow your movements to be transmitted directly to the ski, particularly for edging. As a beginner, comfort is of utmost importance so avoid any pressure points on the foot. When trying on boots, use the same type of sock that you will wear when skiing which should be smooth and not very thick. Do not be tempted to use two pairs; your boot should be warm and comfortable enough without this and two pairs reduces your ability to transmit actions through the foot to the ski.

Balance

You may have found when practising your sliding and stepping exercises that your balance lets you down, so pause for a breather and then try some exercises to help improve this very important aspect of learning to ski.

1 To improve your balance try standing on one ski, first with poles on the ground and then with poles lifted off the ground.

2 Try hopping on two skis first with poles for support and then without.

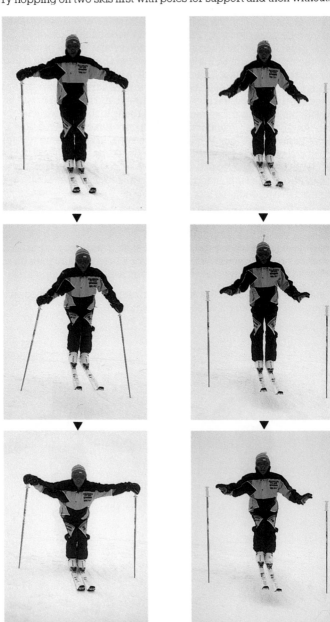

3 Try hopping on one ski first with poles and then without. Make the hops small.

You should now be getting the feel of the skis, and getting to know where to stand to stop the skis sliding away from you either forwards or backwards. The optimum position is right over the middle of the skis.

Now let's look at the best way to stand on skis; we'll call this our basic position.

Basic position

In skiing we need to flex the following areas of the body, starting from the feet up.

1 Ankle joints
These are encased in boots, so to flex them forward you need to press your shins against the front of the boots; this is why it is important to get boots which are not too stiff. Try flexing against the front of the boots and see if you can feel, hear, or see the plastic bending.

2 Knee joints

The knees must come forward as well as the ankles; you can flex the ankles without flexing the knees – however it's easier and correct to flex the knees and ankles together. It is also possible to flex the knees and not the ankles but this leaves you in a sitting down position which is very tiring on the legs, presses your calves into the back of the boots, and does not put you in a good position for controlling your skis.

3 Hip and waist joints

These are important joints in skiing. The pelvic girdle must be tilted upwards and the hip/waist joint is rounded. To get the feeling of rounding the small of the back get someone to put their hand at the back of your waist, then push against it with that part of your spine whilst pulling your tummy muscles in tightly. Tight tummy muscles and a rounded spine are also helpful in absorbing the shock impact caused when we ski, and in avoiding a bad back!

4 Shoulders

Moving up the spine, slightly round the upper back and shoulders. This should automatically happen as you round the small of the back/pelvic girdle giving a continuous curve for the whole of the spine.

Your head should remain up and looking ahead, with the eyeline horizontal.

Your arms should be relaxed and carried away from the body and forward – with the poles slightly diverging at the back.

Keep your skis about hip width apart for stability and balance; get a friend to try pushing you over from the side – if you stand relaxed with feet apart this should prove difficult.

Exercises for basic position

On the spot

1 Imagine yourself as a goalkeeper facing a penalty kick. You are ready
  to move to one side or the other very quickly, your hands are slightly in
  front of you and out to the side. You are flexed and in a ready position.

2 Picture a plumb line dropping from the top of your spine; it should fall
   through the centre of your foot.

On the move

1 Try rocking backwards and forwards as you are gliding on the straight. Find a position that feels good.

2 Bring your hands backwards and forwards. Find a position that feels good.

3 Take your arms out to the side and back in close to your body. Find a
  position that feels good.

Falling

When you fall, and we all do whilst learning to ski, whether you fall on the flat, or later on a slope, try falling to the side and sitting down. Keep your hands up so you don't land with all your weight on them.

If you fall on the flat, it will probably be easier to take off one ski and get up, than to exhaust yourself trying to get up with two skis on.

If you fall on a slope, put your skis below you, and across the slope, so that you don't set off before you are ready. From a sitting position, push off with your uphill hand and roll up to a standing position.

Your poles might be of help. Try it and see; most people seem to develop their own patented method of getting up from a fall, and unfortunately practice is the best way to find out what works for you.

GAINING CONFIDENCE
More exercises to try on the flat

On the spot

1 Plant your poles firmly out to the side, standing with your skis hip width apart – now keeping the tips where they are, hop the tails out so that they are wide apart. This is called a snowplough position. Hop back to a straight 'running' stance and repeat, making the gaps between the tails of your skis vary from small to large.

As an extra, try this without support from the poles.

2 From a basic stance lift one ski into the air. Now practise tapping the tip on the ground as you hum a rhythmic tune (you could practise this once in a while in lift queues if you are brave enough). Try this without support from the poles too.

On the move

From a sliding walk

1 Step out of the direction of travel to avoid an obstacle, for instance a ski pole; then do a complete 360° turn around the obstacle if you can.

2 Skating is a useful manoeuvre to learn on your skis, it will carry you nicely up gentle hills, speed you up on the flat, and help to develop your balance and your edge control.

Skating on skis is much like roller or ice skating, you should lean forward and push off from one ski, and onto the inside edge of the other ski, transferring all your weight to this ski. Next push off on the other ski in the same way. Use your poles for extra impetus.

The key to skating is not to push off too far, but to make small skating steps and learn to ride each one until its speed runs out.

Skiing is about moving, so do as much walking about and experimenting in your beginners' area as possible.

From straight running to snow plough turns

Now that you have mastered walking on the flat and the basic exercises, it's time to let gravity give you a hand. Remember the 'Basic Position' with feet about hip width apart in a comfortable stable stance, and flexed at all the skiing joints, ankles, knees, hips, and waist. Bounce up and down a few times to feel flexed and relaxed. Hold your arms and hands away from your sides and forward to help your balance.

Side stepping up

Now look for a gentle slope with a flat and safe runout. Sidestep up this slope for about 10 steps or so. Sidestepping is just like walking sideways up a staircase, facing the wall or handrail.

If you feel yourself slipping sideways down the slope, push your knees in towards the slope as you step. This will give you a good platform from which to make you next step.

Use your poles to help your balance; plant them in the snow as you make your first step with your uphill leg, then bring your lower leg up to join it. Now stand on this downhill leg, making sure your knee is pushed in

towards the hill. This will stop you slipping down again. Then lift your poles and uphill leg together and step up. Repeat this until you feel you have gained enough height. (When you get a good rhythm, count the number of steps you make before each downhill run, so that you can increase your run every time as your confidence increases). At the top of your slope, relax to get your breath back.

Straight running down

Look at your proposed route down and make sure there are no obstructions. Place your poles in the snow below you.

Your poles should be about shoulder width apart. If you put your palms on top of the poles and your arms straight like an extension of the pole, you will be able to support your body weight until you are ready to slide down the hill. Make a 90° 'step turn' to point down the hill with your skis pointing

between your poles in the direction you wish to go. Take the strain and lean on your poles, now relax and off you go gliding down the hill on to the runout at the bottom. To stop, make very small steps around, until you come to a standstill. If your practice slope has a gentle runout, all the better, you won't need to do anything except stay in balance until you run out of steam.

Exercises to try when straight running

1 Touch your boots and stand up again.

2 Make a series of small jumps.

3 Lift each ski alternately and put it down again.

4 Step to a new downhill line, stepping one ski across and then the other. (Don't try to take too big a step).

5 Pick up a glove from the snow while moving.

DON'T
Don't: Look at your skis   . . .
Don't: Tense up   . . .
Don't: Lose your balance . . .

DO
Look where you're going
Stay relaxed
Stand on both feet, and flex your
skiing joints

So far you have been 'schussing' (running) down the hill with little or no
control of your speed, and using the run-out to stop. The next step is to
learn how to control your speed and stop when you want to. To do this
we use the snowplough.

You may have to do this part straight away if you cannot find a slope with
a suitable run-out.

Snowplough

To make a snowplough you displace the tails or backs of the skis
outwards, while keeping the tips or fronts of the skis as close as they were

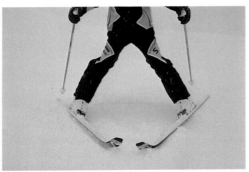

in the straight running position. This automatically brings the skis onto their inside edges, which offers more resistance to your speed. Basically this means that you slow down. Make sure your skis don't go too far onto their inside edges as this will cause the skis to track across each other. Just

push your knees out a little, thereby flattening the skis and reducing any tendency to cross. You should notice that the wider the snowplough the greater the resistance, and therefore the slower you go.

Now sidestep up the hill again as before, step around using your poles for support and set yourself up in a narrow snowplough position. Check again,

are you flexed at all the skiing joints? Are you relaxed? If so then off you go in a fairly narrow gliding plough, and notice that you should be travelling slower than in the straight running position. A few metres down the slope push out the ski tails and sink down a little into a braking plough which should bring you to a complete stop. If you find yourself drifting to one side or the other, then try to equalise the pressure on both skis, bounce up and down a little and experiment with your position, rock from side to side, push your knees in and out, and see what happens.

Exercises to improve snowplough glide and brake

1 From a gliding plough sink down into a braking plough. Look at the two photos, bottom of page 52.

2 Do a series of these, going down to brake and up to glide.

3 Hold your poles in front of you as if carrying a tray of drinks and repeat exercise 2.

4 Use gloves or sticks as markers and try to halt by these as you brake, then narrow to a glide to set off again towards your next 'check point'. You could set yourself a course with your poles, as in the photos.

Going up

Fortunately we no longer have to climb the mountains before skiing down as ski enthusiasts did at the beginning of the century. Resorts have built networks of lifts to take skiers up so they can ski down to catch another lift up. Often neighbouring resorts have linked together to make a larger ski area.

You are likely to come across the following types of lift:

Rope tow

A moving rope with handles attached which you grab to pull you along. Luckily only found on fairly shallow slopes because it gets tiring to hold on.

Drag or button lift

A small round disk ('button') on a shaft which you put between your legs. The shaft is attached to a moving overhead cable which pulls you up a prepared track on your skis. **Do not sit down**. Lean against the disk and hold the shaft as you stand balanced with both sticks in one hand and skis apart in the track. Sometimes as you start you take your own 'button', but in most cases it will be handed to you when you are in the right position.

To get off, take the 'button' from between your legs using the shaft, and push it away from you at the top as you glide to one side.

T bar

Similar to a button lift but takes two people side by side who stand against an anchor shaped fixture again attached to a moving cable. When getting off one person skis to one side and the other gets rid of the T-bar as for the button lift.

Chairlift

A chair hanging on a moving cable suspended between pylons. Prepare yourself in the path of the chair holding your poles in the inside hand. When it comes up behind you catch the outer arm of the chair with the other, outside hand and sit down. Be sure to catch it firmly with your hand before it comes up or it will hit your calves from behind! Chairs usually have a safety bar which you pull down, and a foot rest for your feet (there are less of these in America). Varying types of chairlift take up to four people. They can be cold in bad weather. To get off, take up the safety bar, the chair then lowers you until your skis are touching the snow, then you ski down and out of the way.

Use your hand to push off with when leaving the chairlift.

Gondola

Skiers get into an enclosed cabin, where they either sit or stand. Different sizes take up to ten people. With small ones (up to six people) the skis are carried on racks outside, and in larger ones you take them inside with you.

Cable Car

A large gondola lift suspended on a cable between pylons. These cabins carry up to 150 people and move much faster than gondolas but run less frequently.

Funicular

A mountain railway with separate carriages, mainly found in Switzerland. Skiers usually stand, but if the carriage is not too full seats can be pulled down.

In high season, at the beginning of the day, when ski school starts or at crucial link lifts, there may be lift queues. Like traffic jams, the best way to cope with them is to retain your cool: do not get upset but keep attentive. Try not to stamp on the skis of the person in front or they'll get annoyed, and saving places for other people is frowned upon.

Coming down

Pistes

Ski routes are marked runs down a 'piste'. A piste is a carefully marked area of snow which has been smoothed and prepared by machines ('snow cats') to create a route. In addition, safety is observed: areas of exposed rock are marked and the pylons that hold up lifts are padded. At the end of the day ski patrollers ski down each piste to make sure that no-one has fallen, been injured and left unnoticed. If you ski 'off piste' the run will not be patrolled. This option is *only* for good skiers because the snow will not have been prepared by a snow cat and natural hazards are unmarked.

Pistes are marked according to their difficulty by coloured poles or signs.

Black	very difficult
Red	difficult
Blue	easy
Green	very easy (not all resorts use green)

ON THE SLOPES

During the day you will be bound to get hungry and thirsty because skiing takes a fair bit of energy and the mountain air is very dry. Those on diets will have to abandon ideas of living off a lettuce leaf – it just won't be enough, and could be dangerous. Eat enough, which doesn't mean stuffing yourself with croissants, chips and pastries! Start the day with a good breakfast and drink enough – carry a snack in your pocket.

Mountain restaurants

When it comes to lunch time you'll be starving. Most ski areas have mountain restaurants or self service cafés where there are also toilets. If you are on a tight budget some restaurants allow you to eat a picnic outside but get very annoyed if you take up an inside table for this. You'll certainly pay more for a table with service but it is a nice treat for the last day or when the weather is foul. Most times you'll want to get out on the slopes again but don't underestimate the need for a rest – a hot drink mid morning and again in the afternoon is a good idea. A reasonable lunch in a self service café will cost you an average of £6 per day.

A crowded restaurant, (particularly in or near the village) is a target for ski thieves. To minimise the chance of your equipment being stolen separate your skis. Give one to a friend and take one of theirs to stick in the snow together during lunch. A thief is unlikely to want an odd pair.

Alcohol

Drinking enough liquid does not mean drink alcohol! By all means have a beer, wine or a glass of schnapps, but *don't* go down the slope roaring drunk. You may end up taking runs far above your standard in your enthusiasm, but far worse, you could cause an accident and be rightly sued for negligence.

When to stop

At the end of the day, when you feel tired, stop. Don't be encouraged to ski another run; it could be the one on which you fall and hurt yourself because you are racing to keep up with faster friends and are just too tired.

Snowplough turns

The next stage is learning to use your snowplough technique to turn.

Notice the inside edge of each ski when in a snowplough. If you look at the line of the edge from tail to tip, and imagine a continuation of this, the line from your left ski would be pointing to the right, and the line from your right ski would be pointing to the left . . . If we press on these edges individually we turn in the direction that they are pointing.

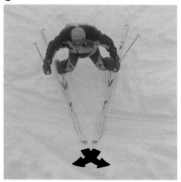

Let's try this out; stand on the inside edge of, say, your left ski and release the pressure a little from your right foot. You should now begin to make a gentle turn to your right. Now equalise the pressure again, you should automatically begin to drift down the 'fall line' (the 'fall line' is your original direction of travel straight down the slope). Now stand on the inside edge of your right ski, and release the pressure from your left foot slightly; this should start you turning to your left.

Exercises to improve your turning

1 Try a series of small pushes on each foot to initiate a turn.

2 Try one push to the count of 3 to initiate a turn.

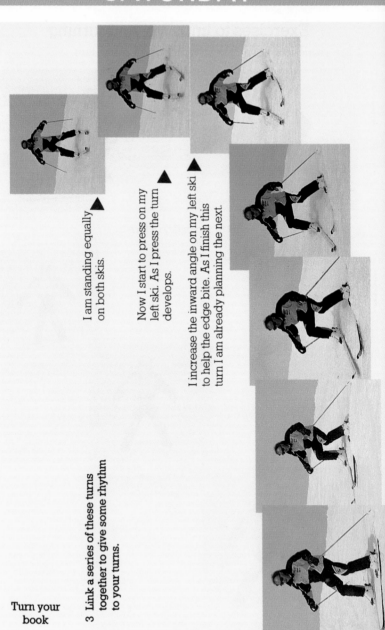

I am standing equally on both skis.

▲

Now I start to press on my left ski. As I press the turn develops.

▲

I increase the inward angle on my left ski to help the edge bite. As I finish this turn I am already planning the next.

Turn your book

3 Link a series of these turns together to give some rhythm to your turns.

I relax, equalise the pressure and stand on both skis which brings me into the fall line.

I start to press on the right ski.

I increase the pressure to develop the turn. I feel the edge bite and start to plan the next turn.

Turn your book

4 Turn around a series of slalom poles.

Stand with equal pressure on both skis, and hands on knees.

Round your back to make sure your bottom doesn't stick up in the air. (It should not be your highest point!)

Now press down harder with your left hand to initiate the turn.

Turn your book

5 **With hands on knees, fine tune your snowploughs.**

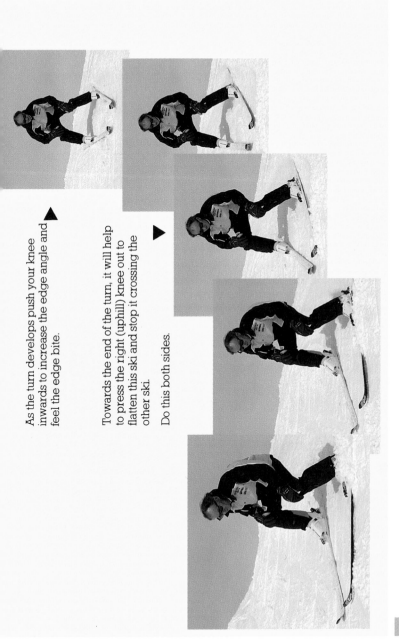

As the turn develops push your knee inwards to increase the edge angle and feel the edge bite. ▶

Towards the end of the turn, it will help to press the right (uphill) knee out to flatten this ski and stop it crossing the other ski. ▶

Do this both sides.

Snowplough turns to stem turns

Now its time to extend your horizons. Practise snowplough turns in full runs; this will help to build up your stamina and will get you around the resort, if you stick to blue or easy runs.

On more gentle slopes vary the radius of the turns by varying the amount of pressure you apply to the ski.

REMEMBER gentle pressure makes for a longer, gentler turn while firm pressure makes for a tighter turn.

Try a run making quicker turns, staying closer to the fall line and generally facing down the hill – you should find that the width of your snowplough will decrease and eventually, with speed and practice, will disappear, and your skis will run parallel.

REMEMBER not to over-edge the ski at slow speeds or it will track across the tip of the other ski.

As you press on the turning or outside ski of the turn focus on removing pressure from the non-turning or inside ski of the turn.

REMEMBER you are trying to flow down the mountain so movements must be in harmony, both internally within your body, and externally with the mountain. Think of a river flowing and going with the terrain – picking the route of least resistance. This should encourage good snow contact and smooth flowing movements, and you will feel nicely relaxed.

As your technique, use of skis, and speed of travel increase, skiing should become easier; and if you have given a little commitment to the suggested practice exercises your progress through the beginner stage will have been quite rapid.

The traverse

You may find as you ski more that you need to get from one area to another travelling directly across the slope, and that a snowplough turn won't do. Travelling across slopes is known as traversing, and the way to proceed is as follows. As you finish one snowplough turn, instead of equalising the pressure and standing evenly on both feet – relax, leave more pressure on the downhill ski and allow the uphill ski to drift in towards the lower one.

To allow it to slide in smoothly you will need to change from the inside to the outside edge of the uphill ski. Think of pushing the top knee uphill and bending the uphill ankle and knee.

As soon as the skis are parallel and hip width apart you are traversing across the slope. Make sure you practise this in both directions until you feel equally in control whichever way you are facing.

Exercises for the traverse

1 Do a body check:
   Is your upper ski slightly ahead?
   Is your upper knee ahead?
   Is your upper hip ahead?
   Is your upper shoulder ahead?
   Is your upper hand ahead?
   Are you looking where you are
   going?
   Are you flexed at all the skiing
   joints as in the basic stance?
   Are your skis hip width apart?

2 Traverse across the slope and lift the tail of the uphill ski off the snow –
   see how far you can ski like this; it will improve your balance.

3 Traverse across the slope and hop both tails off the snow.

4 Traverse across the slope and hold your hands in front of you as if you were the driver of a big bus with a big horizontal steering wheel.

REMEMBER to make sure you don't become a one sided skier, by practising all exercises equally to both sides.

Stem turns

The stem turn is back in fashion. It has been adapted in technique to make it appropriate for today's modern and precise ski equipment, and is an extremely useful bridge between the snowplough and the parallel turn. It will encourage you to maintain a good body position throughout the turn with less tendency to over rotate. At the same time it helps give a solid edge change and promotes maximum use of the new turning edge.

Let's see how it feels.

Turn your book

Starting from a relaxed traverse position, slide or stem out the tail of your uphill ski until you find its inside edge.

Stand on it; it will now begin to turn towards and through the fall line.

As the ski turns through the fall line increase the pressure on it and decrease the pressure on the non-turning ski. When the turn is well under way encourage the non-turning ski to come in parallel, in the same way as you did to get into a traverse.

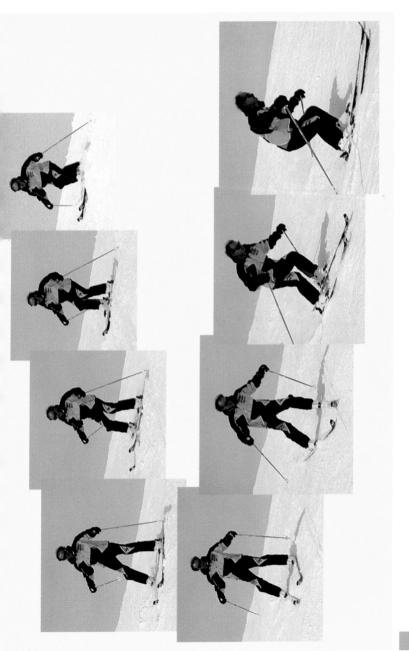

Exercises for the stem turn

We can look at the stem turn in three phases:

1 Initiation.
2 Turning.
3 Finishing.

Let's try some exercises to practise the different phases of the turn:

Initiation

1 Standing still in a traverse position, on a gentle slope, use your poles for support and slide out the uphill ski onto its inside edge. Repeat this on both sides until you are happy that you can slide smoothly, and successfully find the new turning edge.

2 To put number 1 into action try moving in a gentle traverse, and sliding out the uphill ski a few times. Don't stand on it yet, just get the feeling of standing balanced on the inside edge of your downhill ski, and sliding out the uphill ski.
Do this to both sides.

3 Once again pick a wide gentle slope and set off in a traverse. Slide out the upper ski, this is about to become the new turning ski. As soon as you find the inside edge stand firmly on it. You will begin to turn towards the fall line. When you reach the fall line, and before completing the turn, release the pressure on this ski, and re-apply pressure to the old turning ski to bring you back into a traverse in your original direction. Repeat this sequence as many times as you can fit in, in one traverse.

This type of repetitive sequence is known as a garland exercise.

Turning and Finishing

All movements should aim to be flowing, and pressure changes should where possible be gradual. When turning, movements should not be jerky or rushed: let the skis do the work and allow the upper body to flow along naturally.

Here is an exercise which will help you flow:

Standing Still

Flex forward at the ankle, knee, and hip, and become aware of your shin pressing against the front of your boot. Now work out a scale of this pressure. Call the position where your shin is just about touching the front of your boot 'zero'; now flex forward until your shin is putting light to medium pressure on the boot, call this 'one'; let 'two' be medium to strong pressure. This gives you a scale of pressure from zero to two.

On the Move

Try out your scale on the move as follows; from a traverse stem out the
uphill ski, as you find the new edge call out zero to yourself. As the ski
begins to turn feel for 'one' (light to medium pressure on the front of the
boot) as the turn develops and the inside ski slides in feel for 'two'
(medium to strong pressure). Experiment with the timing of this pressure –
for a long gentle turn go from 'zero' to 'two' slowly, for a shorter radius,
more active turn go from 'zero' to 'two' quickly and feel the difference.

Make a turn as above, thinking about your pressure scale as you move through the turn. When you feel that the turn is established start to reach out with your outside arm (the one on the same side as the turning ski). Reach down fairly low, but be careful to reach sideways and down – not forwards and down. This will help you to develop the correctly balanced posture as you make and finish your turns. It will also help you not to overturn.

Start the reach out earlier and earlier in the turn until you start to reach at the very moment that you make the stem. By doing this you are encouraging the soonest possible introduction of the new turning edge.

Snowplough turns allowed you to ski most blue runs in comfort. The stem turn allows you to ski most red or intermediate runs in comfort. As you ski more runs using the stem turn it's possible to work on reducing the stem phase of the turn. Simply skiing a little faster is perhaps one of the easiest and best ways to achieve this. Skiing faster means that you can more easily pressure the uphill or new turning ski, earlier in the turn, and release the pressure on the downhill or old turning ski, earlier. All this allows you to ride the edge of the turning ski from before the fall line to the end of the turn. This is more precise turning, offers more control, and is known as 'carving'.

At slower speeds, when the forces pulling you to the outside of the turn were low, you needed the non-turning ski to act as a stabiliser and stop you falling into the hill. However, as your speed increases so does the force pulling you to the outside of the turn, and your dependence on this stabiliser decreases. The non-turning ski will now drift in to join the turning ski, leading to a parallel turn.

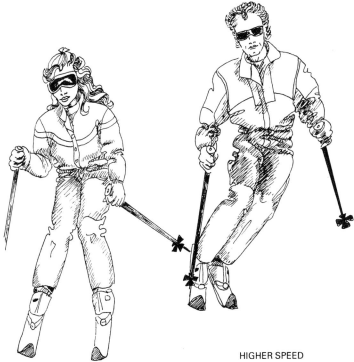

SLOWER SPEED
The non turning ski acts as a stabiliser.

HIGHER SPEED
Pull to the outside of the turn increases, and the stabiliser – no longer needed – drifts in to join the turning ski.

By skiing more, and getting a better 'feel' for your edges you will be able to refine the stem turn, finding the edge and carving earlier in the turn, and more efficiently. If you have also worked on developing your balance the non-turning ski will ride along with the turning ski, and the result is a very pleasing experience – a carved parallel turn.

A word here about 'angulation', which simply explained is the posture that the body adopts relative to the ski in counteracting the forces of the turn. As speed and consequently the force pulling to the outside of the turn increases, the body must counteract this force as precisely as our skill allows. If we cannot adapt our posture correctly we fall over if we over edge the ski, or make a broad skid if we do not have enough edge through the turn.

Here Ian is doing the reaching out exercise, which allows you to see his 'angulation'.

MORE ADVANCED EXERCISES

Side-slipping

Side-slipping, as the name implies, is slipping or skidding sideways down a slope. It is a very useful manouevre, used by skiers at all levels, for descending a slope which is too icy or steep to turn on, or to lose height without travelling too far across a slope. It is an excellent way to extend your ability to ski more varied terrain, but should be viewed as a compromise, albeit an essential one, where edged skis are not appropriate.

Side-slipping is defined under two headings:
1 Vertical side-slip – normally starting from a static position.
2 Diagonal side-slip – from a moving traverse.

The Vertical Side-slip

From a wide stance traverse position on a moderately steep slope, advance the upper ski slightly and turn your upper body, from the hips, to face down the slope. Lift your poles and as you turn your shoulders to face down the slope use your poles for support and for pushing off, this also keeps them out of your way.

To release the edges and initiate the side-slip sink down, flex the ankles, knees and hips, and allow the knees to relax from the traverse position by rolling, or pushing them, out away from the slope slightly. As soon as the edges are released you should find yourself sliding down the slope.

From below:

From the side:

To stop the side-slip stand up and reset the edges by pushing the knees back into the slope again.

Exercises for vertical side-slipping

1 Stand in a traverse on a moderate slope, and place your poles in the snow on either side of you as wide apart as is comfortable.

Step your uphill ski up to your upper pole, and bring your lower ski up to join it; keeping your poles in the snow for support.

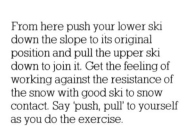

From here push your lower ski down the slope to its original position and pull the upper ski down to join it. Get the feeling of working against the resistance of the snow with good ski to snow contact. Say 'push, pull' to yourself as you do the exercise.

2 From the same position, instead of pushing and pulling down, try releasing both edges simultaneously to slide down to your starting position. Remember to sink as you initiate the slide, and stand over the centre of your skis to press the front and back equally.

3 Stand in the vertical side-slipping position, that is, upper body turned from the hips down the slope, and place your poles in the snow behind you up the slope, from where they are well placed to help you push off to initiate a side-slip.

4 Stand as before, initiate the side-slip by sliding your skis forwards and backwards to release the edges as you flex down.

Diagonal side-slipping

From a wide stance traverse, across a moderate slope, sink down – by flexing the ankles knees and hips – and release the edges slightly to initiate the slip. Keep the upper body (from the hips up) facing your diagonal direction of travel, and allow the legs to turn under you. Stand up to reset the edges and continue the traverse.

Exercises to improve diagonal side-slipping

Do these exercises to left and right.

1 From a gentle traverse, shuffle your feet back and forwards a little to release the edges as you sink down. Face your direction of travel with shoulders and hips. Look at the photos for exercise 4, vertical side-slipping.
2 Initiate the side-slip with a small hop to release the edges.

3 Use a small bump to help get you sliding, by turning your legs as you are on top of the bump.

85

Swing to the hill

If at the end of a diagonal side-slip, instead of standing up to reset the edges, you flex the ankles and knees further forwards and gently re-set the edges by pressing the knees back into the hill, you should now begin to turn uphill. This is called a swing to the hill, which is useful for stopping, or regaining edge control after side-slipping or skidding. When used with a good degree of edging a swing to the hill is like the finishing phase of a turn.

Try this from a gentle traverse by sinking down (do not release the edges as you do when sideslipping) and press forward against the front of your boots. You will begin to turn uphill. Allow the upper body to follow the skis, rather than to lead, and so remain square to the direction of travel. The radius of the swing will vary as the pressure varies; as always, gentle pressure will cause a gentle long radius turn or swing, while hard pressure will give a shorter radius swing.

Read the photo sequence from the top of page 87 . . . ▶

Exercises for swing to the hill

1 **Vary the traverse** line from shallow to steep.

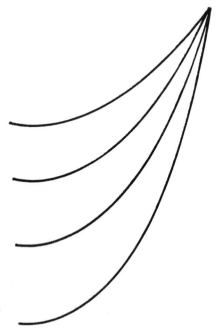

2 Hop into the swing: from a traverse, hop the tails of the skis off the snow, as you land flex forward and press into the front of your boots.

3 Reach out with the lower hand. This will help you to keep your edges set and stop you side-slipping.

Safety

For the full enjoyment of a skiing holiday, safety on the slopes is of paramount importance. For the safety of others and your own sake heed the following code of conduct. It is important to ski with respect for the mountains and those who live there, to maintain the good reputation of British skiers abroad.

FIS Code of conduct

1 Respect for others
   A skier shall conduct himself in such a way that he does not endanger
   or prejudice others.
2 Speed and way of skiing
   A skier must adapt his speed and his way of skiing to his personal
   ability as well as to prevailing general conditions.
3 Choice of course
   A skier coming from above must choose his course in such a way that
   he assures the security of the skier below.
4 Overtaking
   It is permitted to overtake another skier, going down or up, to the right
   or to the left, but a wide margin must be given to the skier being
   overtaken to permit him to make his turns.
5 Obligations for skiers further down and skiers crossing the piste
   A skier wishing to enter a downhill piste or cross such a piste must by
   looking up and down assure himself that he can do so without danger to
   himself or others. The same goes for a skier starting after a stop on the
   piste.
6 Stopping on the piste
   A skier must avoid, if not absolutely necessary, stopping at narrow
   passages or places with bad visibility. After a fall, the skier must as
   soon as possible leave such places.
7 Climbing
   A climbing skier must use only the side of the piste. In bad visibility he
   cannot even do this. The same goes for a skier who is going down on
   foot.
8 Respect for the signs
   Every skier must respect the signs on downhill pistes.
9 Conduct at accidents
   At accidents everybody is duty-bound to assist.
10 Identification
   Everybody who is a witness, responsible or not in an accident, is
   required to establish his identity.

Adhere to the above for your safety. If you are seen to be wilfully ignoring
this code of conduct and thus cause an accident you will be held
responsible.

At the end of the day

'Après ski' can play an important part in a ski holiday but it has to be taken
in moderation because too much night life leaves little energy for skiing.

From the moment your skis are taken off it is après ski time. Peruse the
shops of Courmayeur, or wander the streets of Cortina. Have a crepe in

SUNDAY

Val d'Isère, an ice cream coupe in Klosters or chocolate torte in St Moritz, a gluhwein in St Anton or a glass of schnapps in Kitzbühel – all are part and parcel of a skiing holiday evening out. In the Tyrolean resorts of Austria Tea Dancing is popular. It's off with the skis and straight into a bar for drinks and dancing (ski boots stay on so dancing is often rather a clumping affair).

Most people, however, will find that a drink on the way home is all they immediately have energy for – post skiing 'putting your feet up' is an important part of the holiday. All that fresh air and exercise combined with the warmth of the hotel will almost certainly make you nod off.

More activity

Once you have recovered, showered and changed it is time to take your light from under the bushel: for instance, there is nothing like an hour of fun on an ice rink for gaining an appetite. If it is watching, not participating, that appeals to you, a chance to watch a local ice hockey match should not be missed. The atmosphere is electric as padded wonders speed up and down the icy pitch. Many resorts offer the chance to go night tobogganing – or do even more skiing. Torch lit descents of the slopes are usually arranged through the ski school or tour operator Reps and take place after a dinner up on the mountain.

Eating out

Throughout the Alps local specialities have developed, partially due to the fact that in the past complete areas or valleys were cut off by snow and so the locals developed ways of spending time over their food and making it more interesting. Dairy products and meats dominate.

Traditionally the fondue or raclette (the melted scrapings of a slab of cheese eaten with boiled potatoes) are dishes associated with a skiing holiday. Preparing these yourself can be fun. There are many variations on the theme now, with different flavours added to cheese, and meat cooked in either oil (fondue bourgignonne) or a delicious stock (fondue Chinoise).

For many the night doesn't even end at dinner. In the larger traditional resorts bars and night clubs are popular if expensive, and the ubiquitous disco has sprung up everywhere. There is something to suit everyone but research is needed to find out where it is!

Enjoy your skiing!

With a little commitment to learning, and an interest in what is happening under your feet, the possibility is strong that you will rapidly achieve the status of a parallel skier. But more importantly, by following the exercises in this book you will develop a sensitivity to each individual ski. This ability to feel what is happening is known as 'independent leg action', something which is often lost after the snowplough stage in many ski school courses and you should also have a greater feel for your edges than most other skiers at your level.

We hope that we have set you on the piste towards a happy, lifelong relationship with your skis!